BOATING with BUDDY

EPISODE 1

A special report from our canine correspondent in the Pacific Northwest

By **Buddy**, a beagle mix rescue dog
with Susan Specht Oram

Let me introduce myself...

My name is Buddy the rescue dog. I'm part Beagle and I have a curly tail. (You'll see my tail featured in a few photos later on.)

I had one of my humans put this book together about my adventures, since I can't type. I'm waiting for someone out there to invent a paw-friendly keyboard. (Will one of you please do that??)

I've tried to be an impartial observer in my capacity as your foreign correspondent, reporting in from the Pacific Northwest and British Columbia, Canada. Our pack has been out on a boat. We've seen a lot of water. And, I've smelled many delectable scents on beaches, which you'll see in the pages ahead.

I will caution you that, as a hound, I'm governed by my nose and partial to tangents. We may suddenly jog off to take a turn in the story (like into the bar where I smelled burgers cooking!).

Let's begin with the highlights before we dive into the photos, my riveting commentary and a few tell-all anecdotes. Here is my tail, I mean tale.

It all started when I was wandering down a road in Eastern Washington. Somehow, I ended up in a pack in Seattle. My new girlfriend, Fiona the black lab, lived next door. After a few years, we left Fiona and moved to Anacortes, near what humans call the San Juan Islands. I like the smells here—from food trucks, pubs, ships that give fish to my human and the park where my friends meet to bark and run.

Before we dive into some pretty cool photos (especially ones that feature me! Don't get the wrong impression though, I'm a humble mutt from meager beginnings), you can see here that one of my humans plays the trumpet. It can be pretty loud. I've trained HIM to play with a "mute" to soften the sound he calls "music".

One of my special tricks is to sing along and hit high notes with a little something extra. I don't think he values my sense of music appreciation. But I'm not giving up. These humans are a special project that I've taken on as my life's work.

The "improvement project" for my humans is underway. Frankly, it started when I got the pack out of the house to walk, rain or shine. That's the regimen I recommend. So far, my humans have been malleable and are conforming to the program.

I could write a whole other book about my dogma, for those of you who may be interested. I'm thinking of calling it: "Why I bark, a treatise" or perhaps "My professional career of watching and waiting". Or, this has possibilities, don't you think? "My treatise about dogs and my dogma about treats." Oh wait, that could be: "My treatise about treats and my dogma about dogs"!

In keeping with that philosophical note (and yes, I know we're on a tangent here), I'd like to give a "bark out" here to dogs who need a paw up and are looking for more out of life. This book may inspire some of you canine readers to become pack leader. Here's what I've learned: Humans need furry guidance. We can train them to be their best! Take my people, for instance… With my help, they're out walking 4 times a day. And, they're trained on a leash!

Well, enough about how I came to be with this pack and that jog off into big thinking (I bet some of you didn't know that we dogs muse over lofty topics…). For some reason, my humans decided to get a boat. Really, I thought our land-based existence worked just fine. But no one asked me. I have to admit there is an upside: I specialize in scents and the boat has become a vehicle to arrive at places with new aromas. Let's get on with my special report about boating in the Pacific Northwest!

Your candid canine correspondent, **Buddy**

In this photo, I'm posing with one of my human's musical instruments. I think I look a bit apprehensive…I'd rather go boating than hear trumpet music!

In this pic, I was saying, "Enough of gardening—let's get out on the boat!"

Before I rescued these humans from their dull existence, they went places without me, like to Princess Louisa Inlet in HIS old boat. Without me, I bet it wasn't as much fun ... Now they have lots of fun getting in the dinghy to go to shore. I think I'm a good influence and keep them in shape. If they didn't walk with me, what would they be doing anyway?

It's my job to check for smugglers before we leave the dock!

Here is my regal beagle pic. I try to be at peace on the boat and wait politely for my next meal. I've come a long way from wandering down a road and then being at a shelter in a pen with really BIG dogs who ate all the food . . . did I mention that I love **food?**

Safety first! I have my yellow bumblebee like life jacket on and I'm ready for a dinghy ride with my humans. I love to go ashore and explore the smells. I'm learning to distinguish quite a few new aromas. The poor humans don't know what they're missing...

You never know who might come by on the dock! I'm the designated lookout.
I've been looking for that cat on the sailboat...I know I saw it here last year! Did you say
CAT????

Why can't I go off the leash here, on this beach? Can't you see I need to chase seagulls to boost my self-esteem? It would also be a good workout for me, to stay in shape ... No? I bet I could find something really special to roll around in as a gift for you—like a dead fish?

There IS a cat on a boat—I knew it! I saw it last year at Friday Harbor. It looks pretty big. Maybe it's best if I keep my distance for now... I like cats. They're one of my hobbies.

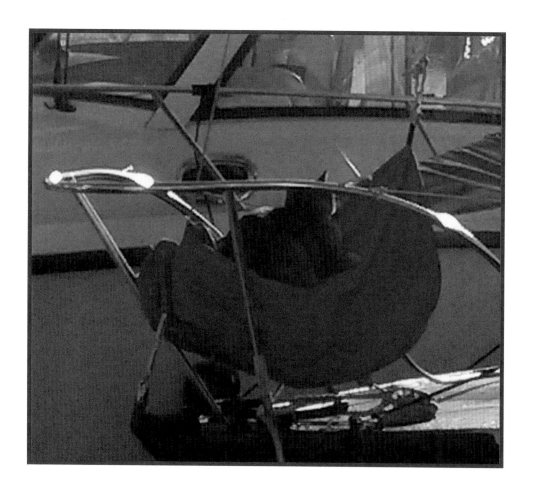

We were anchored for the night in Hunter Bay. Really, I think they should appreciate my prowess at jumping into the dinghy to go for walks! So far, no one has thanked me yet, but I know they secretly like taking me out in the dinghy as dusk settles and just after dawn...

There's one of my humans hanging out with me at West Sound Marina on Orcas Island. Boy, they sure age fast, don't they? I heard there was a great restaurant nearby. I didn't get to go. They also didn't bring back a "doggie bag"... duly noted, humans!

Here we're heading into Fisherman Bay on Lopez Island. What's tough for me is when my humans take **SO LONG** to get to shore. I keep hearing about low tides and rocks, but what's the big deal anyway?

This should give you an idea of why HE was **SERIOUS** as we entered Fisherman Bay. I noticed a dog playing on the beach and considered jumping ship. I'm proud to say, I stayed with my pack. Rabbits hop around the marinas here—there were so many that my friend Echo almost lost her mind. I kept it together, being a more mature mutt and to provide an example of excellent demeanor. But I'll tell you, I could hardly contain myself! It would have been exhilarating, chasing those rabbits, all with little white tails! Tonight, I'll dream about chasing rabbits...

One day, the U.S. Coast Guard came aboard and inspected us. They really liked the fact that I had my yellow life jacket on—not like the humans! They were told to put life jackets on, just like me, while underway. I liked the tall Coast Guard guy. He was very friendly to me.

Waiting for Happy Hour to start . . .

These tugboats sure kick up a big wake. I've developed a method for dealing with it, so I'm all set. I go to the back of the boat—they tell me it's called the "stern" or something—and chill out until I smell land. Then I bark as much as I can on a per minute basis. I think my record was one bark per second as we approached the Reid Harbor dock on Stuart Island. I added a "certain something" to my bark that time!

Here's the lighthouse at Turn Point on Stuart Island. It took a long time for the humans to walk there in the hot sun. They kept talking about interior decorating in the outhouse there . . . who cares about wall art or decorations? I know it smelled like something to stay away from. They looked for whales—that's a big deal for these poor humans. Maybe they need more mental stimulation? Perhaps I can cook something up, like hiding socks . . .

This is a glamour shot as I bask in the sun at Maple Bay Marina. The humans had an electrical problem on board that made it a short cruise today. (I prefer 3-4 hour runs on the boat. They don't know I pushed a button on the inverter to turn it off in order to end today's cruise sooner and stop at a pub . . .)

Are you open for business yet? I can smell something delicious cooking in there. I'm ready for a burger and I think it's time I went into a pub. I'm old enough in dog years—about 50 year's old—for Pete's sake! I can smell the meat cooking!

We're underway here in Desolation Sound. I'm most excited about the new smells that I'll detect at the next stop . . .

I'm at my best when we're underway on the fly bridge! There are so many smells to appreciate. It's like wine tasting for a dog and I have a very discriminating palate for odors at sea.

Refuge Cove didn't have much space for me to walk around. It sure was rich in smells! One of my humans filled our water tanks but there was a break in the water line— we had salt water in the tanks on our boat! I had to drink water from a jug for a while after that. I was a good sport and didn't complain. I try to make them happy. That's part of my job description in this pack, as I see it.

I'm pretty relaxed here leaving Von Donop Inlet. When we went to shore, one of my humans—HER—pulled the dinghy up at low tide and got stuck in the deep mud! We discovered this was NOT the sandy beach it appeared to be ... On our walk, my humans saw signs about **WOLVES!** Of course, I didn't need words to tell me—the musky scent made my hackles go up! Oh my!!

I like to travel with another dog so we can play together when humans take a break. Here's Echo's boat at anchor. I have to say—and I hope she doesn't hear about this—her bark is really high-pitched. Maybe voice training would help her bring it down to a mellow tone, like my hound baying that everyone remarks upon and just loves!

I wasn't real excited about heading to Rebecca Spit, but that was before I smelled a cougar there. And the scent of black bear! I really liked the beach at Rebecca Spit. You might say that Echo and I "frolicked about" there with great merriment…

This is a shot of Secret Cove Marina. It was an OK spot, from my point of view. We had drama when that grandmother fell off the road and down the hill a ways. Echo's human pulled her up from the bushes. I helped by barking a lot. I didn't wait for someone to alert me to my special task in the rescue. I knew right away what to do!

Here's our boat at Secret Cove. I try to customize it from time to time by leaving lots of extra hair around. I wish they'd let me pick what's for dinner each night . . .

I love holidays. And, I'm patriotic on July 4th, even if I'm in Canada on that day. Don't get me started about cannons going off on Canada Day, July 1! That's when I look for a small, quiet space, preferably with a black carpet where I can leave hairs behind to mark my sentiments about the noise.

It gets choppy sometimes and there are lots of boats in the water at the same time. I hear humans talking about "boat traffic" but I think they should listen to me and take turns on the water: One boat at a time, that's my suggestion.

Near Nanaimo we stayed at a dock at Newcastle Island Marine Park. I thought the 5 mile walk around the island was pretty special … I was ready to walk that again the next morning, but my humans had other ideas.

I'm guarding the BBQ. Humans don't appreciate all the work I do before dinner, looking out for their best interests.

Here's yet again another sunset pic. I don't know why my human insisted on including this one. Really, in dog time, sunset is just the time after dinner.

Well, you caught me sleeping here, just chilling out and taking a cat nap. Did someone say Cat? Where? I know a few words, like treat, dinner, breakfast and cat. But seriously, I've learned it's important to take a nap while underway on the boat. That's on my schedule while I wait for my next treat.

I'm looking forward to getting to land in this shot!

I'm happy in this photo, although you can't see me. We're heading for home after being in Desolation Sound. Time to get home and bark at the FedEx and the UPS trucks!!

This is a pretty cool shot, don't you think? Two tugs at the end of our street, with a hint of my tail. It's always good to be home to smell what's new!

Well, that's all for now. My humans really could work on their photo skills to get better photos of me... they'll eventually get it right, I guess. I know they mean well. They could also have more treats on hand. I notice the supply is getting low. I'm going to send them a mind message for MORE DOG TREATS. . . we'll see if they pick up on it. (I also like to stare at them when they're watching TV, just to see what they'll say.)

If you'd like to hear about my new adventures, then email my human HER with "Buddy" in the subject line: spechtoram@gmail.com. (I'm working on a second canine report about boating in the Pacific NW . . .) Bye for now!

Sincerely and very politely,

 Buddy, the regal beagle mix mutt

Your canine correspondent reporting in

from the Pacific Northwest

Interior book design by Rose Michelle Taverniti

Thank you to Deb Welch, who took the first photos of the pub, regal beagle and checking for smugglers. A big bark out to Echo, the black and white rescue dog and boating pal

If you enjoyed reading Boating with Buddy, please recommend it to others and review it on Amazon.com.

Follow Buddy on Facebook: @Buddycaninecorrespondent
On YouTube, search for: Susan Specht Oram with Buddy the boat dog

Made in the USA
Columbia, SC
27 October 2018